ROCKS
Let's Investigate

by Ruth Owen and Victoria Dobney

Consultant:

Nicky Waller

Published in 2019 by Ruby Tuesday Books Ltd.

Editor: Mark J. Sachner
Designer: Emma Randall
Production: John Lingham
Proofreader: Evie Croft

Photo credits:
Alamy: 11 (top right), 18 (top right); Antarctic Program, National Science Foundation/Peter Rejcek: 22 (top); David A. Burnham, University of Kansas: 18 (bottom right); Tom Connell: 19, 20—21; Creative Commons: 5 (top), 24 (top), 25 (centre); James Kuether: 18 (bottom left), 22 (bottom); Ruby Tuesday Books: 10, 15 (bottom), 23; Science Photo Library: 6 (bottom centre), 7 (top right), 12 (bottom), 24 (centre), 25 (top), 27 (top right); Shutterstock: Cover, 1, 2—3, 4, 5 (bottom), 6, 7 (top left), 7 (bottom), 8—9, 11 (top left), 12 (top right), 13, 14, 15 (top), 16—17, 18 (top left), 24 (bottom), 26, 27 (top left), 27 (bottom), 28—29.

ISBN 978-1-78856-035-1

Printed in Poland by L&C Printing Group

www.rubytuesdaybooks.com

Contents

The download button shows there are free worksheets or other resources available. Go to: **www.rubytuesdaybooks.com/scienceKS2**

Our Rocky World Rocks!

Granite

Limestone

Marble

Quartz

Earth is a very rocky place. You can pick up pebbles on beaches and dig up stones in gardens. There are mountains, hills, cliffs and **canyons**. And if you were to dig down and down into the ground, you would always eventually hit rock. Why?

Earth is completely covered with a thick layer of rock called the **crust**. We can't always see the rock because it is under buildings, roads, grass and **soil**.

But when we look at a mountain or the Grand Canyon, we are actually seeing a section of Earth's rocky crust.

Carved By Water

About five million years ago, the Grand Canyon did not exist. There was only a vast area of rocky land. Then the Colorado River started to flow over the land. It took millions of years, but the rushing river water cut down through the rock and carved the famous canyon.

The Grand Canyon is 446 kilometres long. It is 29 km wide at its widest point and in places it is 1.6 km deep.

The Grand Canyon is in Arizona, USA.

Colorado River

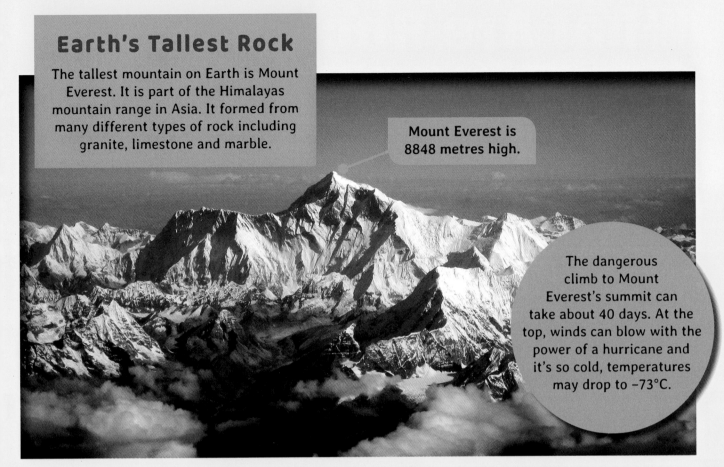

Earth's Tallest Rock

The tallest mountain on Earth is Mount Everest. It is part of the Himalayas mountain range in Asia. It formed from many different types of rock including granite, limestone and marble.

Mount Everest is 8848 metres high.

The dangerous climb to Mount Everest's summit can take about 40 days. At the top, winds can blow with the power of a hurricane and it's so cold, temperatures may drop to −73°C.

There are thousands of different kinds of rocks on Earth.

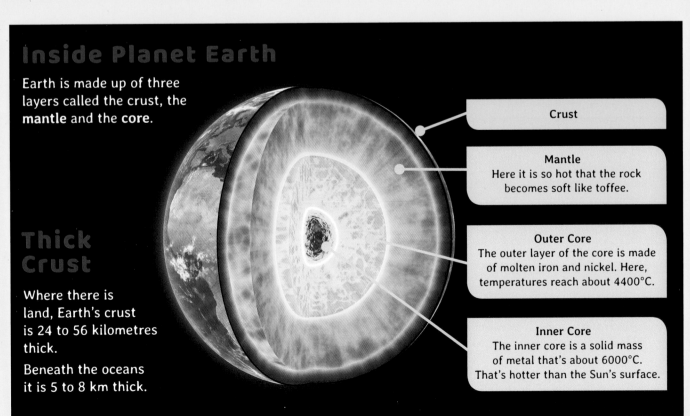

Inside Planet Earth

Earth is made up of three layers called the crust, the **mantle** and the **core**.

Thick Crust

Where there is land, Earth's crust is 24 to 56 kilometres thick.

Beneath the oceans it is 5 to 8 km thick.

Crust

Mantle
Here it is so hot that the rock becomes soft like toffee.

Outer Core
The outer layer of the core is made of molten iron and nickel. Here, temperatures reach about 4400°C.

Inner Core
The inner core is a solid mass of metal that's about 6000°C. That's hotter than the Sun's surface.

What Are Rocks Made Of?

Rocks are made of solid substances called minerals.

Minerals form naturally on Earth and in space. Some rocks form from just one kind of mineral. Others are a mixture of several different kinds.

Some rocks are made from tiny **grains** of minerals. In other rocks the minerals form in shapes called **crystals**. The grains or crystals join together to make solid rock.

A crystal has straight edges and smooth sides called faces.

A quartz crystal

Quartz is one of the minerals in granite rock.

El Capitan

Rock Made of Crystals

El Capitan is a giant granite rock in Yosemite National Park in California, USA. It looks grey, but up close the rock is actually speckled black, grey and white. The granite is made of billions of tiny interlocking crystals of minerals.

Granite up close

There are more than **3000** different minerals on Earth.

Granite crystals viewed with a microscope

Sandstone cliffs in Devon

Rock Made of Grains

When you look through a microscope at sandstone rock you can see grains with a rounded shape. Large grains are held together by smaller grains that act like the cement that joins bricks together in a wall.

Sandstone grains viewed with a microscope

Some kinds of rocks contain metal. That's because metals, such as iron or aluminium, are also minerals that come from the Earth's crust. A rock that contains metal is called an **ore**.

This sandstone rock contains iron. The metal is removed from the rock and used to make steel for manufacturing cars, buses and planes.

Bauxite

Copper is a metal that comes from a rock called chalcopyrite. Nickel comes from a rock called garnierite. Copper and nickel are both used for making coins.

Chalcopyrite

Garnierite

Aluminium for making cans or foil comes from a rock called bauxite.

An ore is heated with chemicals until it melts and the pure metal separates out as a liquid. The liquid metal then cools and hardens.

Igneous Rocks

Scientists and rock collectors sort rocks into three main groups called **igneous rocks, sedimentary rocks** and **metamorphic rocks.** The way that a rock forms tells us which kind it is.

Igneous rocks form from hot, liquid rock called **magma** from inside Earth. How?

Earth's crust is broken into large pieces called **tectonic plates** that fit together like a jigsaw puzzle. The tectonic plates are always slowly moving. As they do, they crunch together and their edges slip under each other. This causes cracks in the crust that allow magma to come to the surface.

The temperature of lava can reach 1000°C – ten times hotter than boiling water.

A **volcano** is a crack in the Earth's crust. When a volcano erupts, magma bursts onto the surface. Once the molten magma is outside of the Earth, it is known as **lava.**

Lava that's cooling

The air cools the flowing lava and it starts to thicken. Eventually it cools completely and becomes solid igneous rock.

Basalt rock formed from lava

Igneous rock can also form inside Earth's crust. Sometimes cracks appear inside the crust deep underground. Magma oozes up into the cracks and slowly cools and hardens, becoming igneous rock.

Pegmatite is an igneous rock that forms underground.

The minerals in igneous rock form as crystals. Igneous rock that forms underground cools slowly over thousands of years, giving the crystals lots of time to grow.

Igneous rock that forms from lava on Earth's surface cools more quickly. Its crystals are tiny, so the rock is often smooth.

The Giant's Causeway

The Giant's Causeway in Northern Ireland is made of an igneous rock called basalt. The columns of basalt formed from magma that erupted from underground about 50 million years ago.

The Giant's Causeway gets its name from an old legend that says it was part of a bridge built by a giant.

Smooth obsidian rock that formed from lava

Sedimentary Rocks

Sedimentary rocks are made from tiny pieces of rock called sediment. How does sediment form?

The process of making sedimentary rock doesn't happen quickly. It can take thousands or millions of years for the layers to build up and rock to form.

1 As rainwater washes over mountains and other rocks, tiny particles of rock, or sediment, break off. This process is called **weathering**.

Sediment

Mountain

2 The sediment may be carried by rainwater into a river and then into a lake or the sea, where it sinks to the bottom. The movement of sediment to a new place is called **erosion**.

Bits of dead animals and plants mix with the sediment, too.

3 Layer upon layer of sediment builds up.

Lake

4 All that sediment, or rock, weighs so much that the layers at the bottom become tightly pressed together. The pressure causes the sediment to actually join and form solid rock.

Layers of sediment

5 In time, the lake or sea dries up, revealing the sedimentary rock.

Solid rock

Sand is a type of sediment.

The layers are different colours because they are made from different types of sediment.

The Old Man of Hoy

Pebbles and sediment weathered from the cliff

The Old Man of Hoy

The Old Man of Hoy, in Scotland, is a tower of sandstone rock that's as tall as a 40-storey building. Sandstone is a type of sedimentary rock. The rocky tower used to be joined to the sandstone cliff behind it. Over hundreds of years, waves crashed into the cliff, weathering and breaking up the rock.

Making New Rock with Wind

Wind can also create sediment in dry places, such as deserts, where there is little water. As wind blows, it picks up loose pieces of sand. The flying sand rubs against large rocks, causing billions of tiny pieces to break off. Over millions of years layers of this sediment build up, join together and make new sedimentary rock.

Metamorphic Rocks

Metamorphic rocks form from other rocks that have been changed by extreme heat or pressure underground. How does this happen?

Sometimes a crack forms underground in Earth's crust. Then super-hot magma oozes into the crack. The extreme heat from the magma bakes the rocks around the crack and changes them.

Metamorphic rock can form underground in another way.

As Earth's tectonic plates move, rocks in the crust get crushed, folded, stretched and rubbed against each other. This causes extreme pressure and heat that bakes the rocks and turns them into metamorphic rocks.

When limestone is baked underground, it changes from a sedimentary rock into a metamorphic rock called marble.

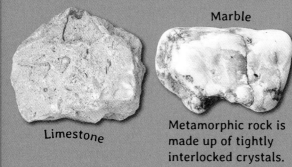

Marble

Limestone

Metamorphic rock is made up of tightly interlocked crystals.

From Granite to Gneiss

This rock is called gneiss. Its swirled pattern shows how it was folded and stretched as it turned from igneous granite into metamorphic gneiss.

All Change

What happens if a metamorphic rock gets baked or crushed? It changes into a new kind of metamorphic rock!

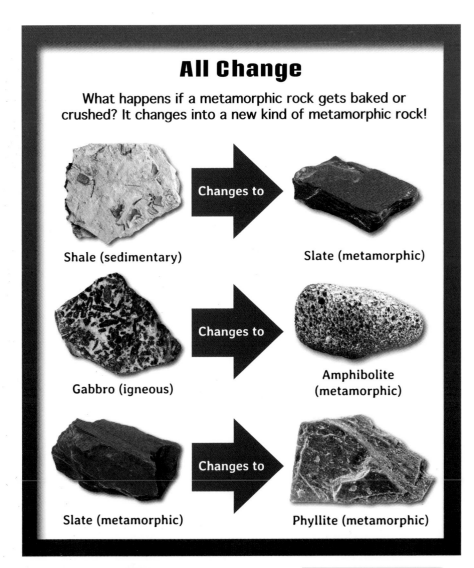

Shale (sedimentary) → **Changes to** → Slate (metamorphic)

Gabbro (igneous) → **Changes to** → Amphibolite (metamorphic)

Slate (metamorphic) → **Changes to** → Phyllite (metamorphic)

When rocks rub together, the pressure and friction create heat. Try this for yourself by pressing the palms of your hands together hard and rubbing them. What do you feel?

The word *metamorphic* comes from the word *metamorphism*, which means "change in form".

This marble formed underground millions of years ago, but now it is at the surface.

At this quarry, giant blocks of marble are being cut from a hillside. The marble will be used to make statues, buildings, floor tiles and kitchen worktops.

Metamorphic rocks form deep underground, so how do we find them?

As wind and rain wear away Earth's surface, the top layers of rock crumble and are blown or washed away. Over millions of years, rocks that were once underground become Earth's new surface layer.

When movements happen in Earth's crust, metamorphic rocks that were deep underground get pushed up to the surface.

The Rock Cycle

Most of the rocks we see around us are millions of years old. But rocks don't stay the same forever. Old rocks are slowly changing into new ones all the time.

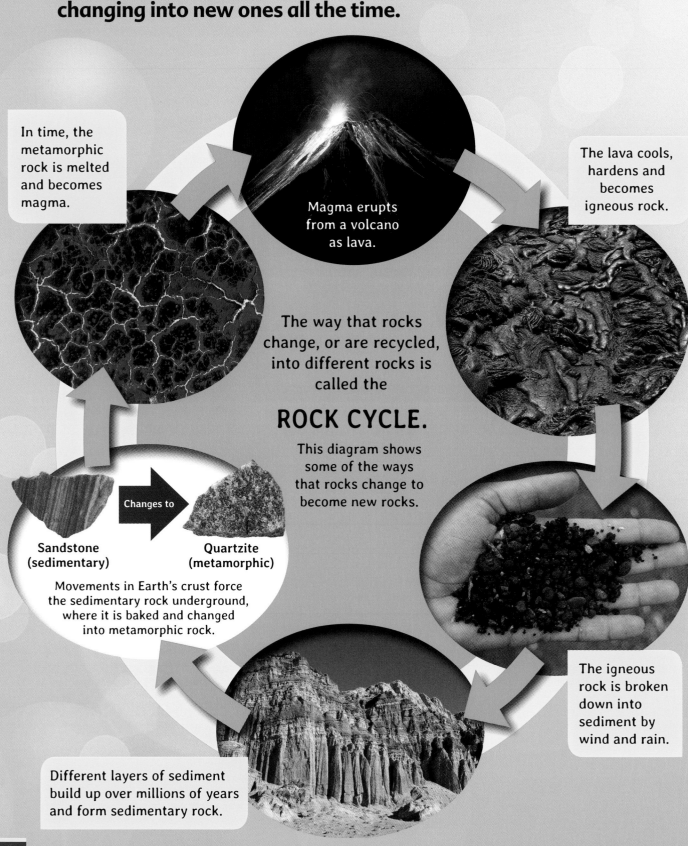

In time, the metamorphic rock is melted and becomes magma.

Magma erupts from a volcano as lava.

The lava cools, hardens and becomes igneous rock.

The way that rocks change, or are recycled, into different rocks is called the

ROCK CYCLE.

This diagram shows some of the ways that rocks change to become new rocks.

Changes to

Sandstone (sedimentary)

Quartzite (metamorphic)

Movements in Earth's crust force the sedimentary rock underground, where it is baked and changed into metamorphic rock.

The igneous rock is broken down into sediment by wind and rain.

Different layers of sediment build up over millions of years and form sedimentary rock.

Making New Rock

The Half Dome rock formation is made of granite, a type of igneous rock that forms underground. The granite formed about 65 million years ago. Then movements of the Earth's crust pushed the granite up to the surface from underground.

Today, wind, rain, snow and even hikers are weathering the rock and turning it to sediment. Millions of years from now, tiny pieces of Half Dome may be inside a cliff or hillside made of sedimentary rock.

Half Dome is in Yosemite National Park in California, USA.

Let's Revise It!

Make a model of the rock cycle and then use it to explain to a friend how the three main types of rocks form.

Make a Rock Cycle Model

Equipment:
• Plasticine
• Stones
• A large piece of cardboard
• Scissors
• White and coloured paper
• A marker pen

Method:

1 Use stones and red plasticine to make an erupting volcano.

2 Then make models in plasticine of the different kinds of rocks.

3 Place your models on the cardboard and make labels and arrows to complete the cycle.

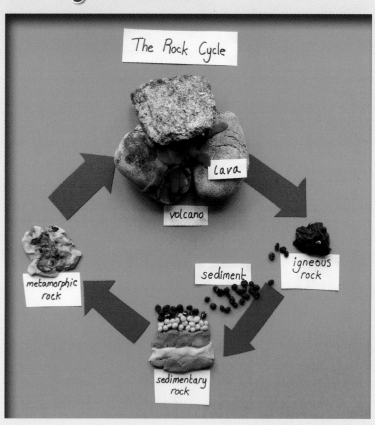

Be a Geologist

The science of studying rocks is called **geology**.
Scientists who study rocks are **geologists**.

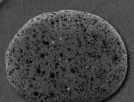

A rock's **properties** help geologists identify it and **classify** it as either igneous, sedimentary or metamorphic.

Rock Words

These words can be used to describe rocks.

rough/smooth
dull/shiny
hard/soft
bumpy/jagged
polished
heavy/light
cold/warm
single coloured
multicoloured
crystalline
(has crystals in it)
grainy
crumbly
sandy
striped/spotty
shimmery
translucent
transparent
flat
rounded
pitted (tiny holes all over it)
absorbent/non-absorbent

Let's Investigate

See if you can find about 10 different rocks, for example in your garden, playground or at the beach. You can also buy rocks online or from a rock collector's shop. Then get investigating!

What are my rocks' properties?

Equipment:
- Your selection of rocks
- A notebook and pen
- Coloured pens or pencils
- A camera or phone
- A ruler
- A magnifying glass or hand lens
- A coin
- Some water and a teaspoon or dropper

Method:

1. Draw a picture of a rock or take a photo, print it out and stick it in your notebook.

2. Measure and record the size of your rock and describe its shape. Now carefully observe your rock and use the list of rock words and the questions below to describe its properties. Record your observations in your notebook.

- Where did you find the rock?
- How do you think it got there?
- How would you describe its colour?
- How does it feel?
- Can you scratch it with your fingernail? (If so, it's soft.)
- Can you scratch it with a coin? (If not, it's hard.)
- If you drop a little water on the rock does it run off or does the rock absorb it?
- Look at the rock under a magnifying glass or hand lens. Can you see grains, crystals, holes or another interesting feature?
- Does it look like any of the rocks on page 17?

3. Now examine another rock. How is it similar to or different from your first rock?

Igneous Rocks

Red granite

Snowflake obsidian

Diorite

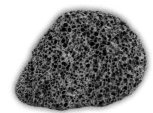
Pumice

Andesite

Peridotite

Scoria

Pegmatite

Sedimentary Rocks

Dolomite

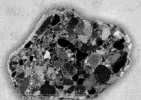
Conglomerate

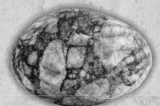
Breccia

Chert

Flint

Banded ironstone

Chalk

Shale

Metamorphic Rocks

Hornfels

Soapstone

Quartzite

Suevite

Jaspillite

Migmatite

Serpentinite

Amphibolite

17

Dinosaurs in Rocks

Rocks can tell us incredible things about Earth's past. That's because some rocks contain fossils.

Fossils are the remains of animals and plants that lived millions of years ago. Scientists called **palaeontologists** have discovered fossilised bones, teeth, horns, footprints, leaves and seeds.

Fresh bone is white, chalky and very light. Fossil bone is dark, shiny and heavy as rock — that's because it has become rock!

Tyrannosaurus rex fossil

A fossilised *T. rex* foot

A Toothy Fossil Clue

In South Dakota, USA, scientists found a fossilised hadrosaur tail bone. It had a broken-off *T. rex* tooth stuck in it. What does this fossil tell us? It tells us that *T. rex* ate hadrosaurs. But did *T. rex* hunt hadrosaurs or **scavenge** on ones that were already dead? Some new bone had grown around the tooth after the attack. This tells us that the hadrosaur was still alive when *T. rex* took a bite, and that the hadrosaur escaped and survived!

A *T. rex* attacking a type of hadrosaur called *Edmontosaurus*

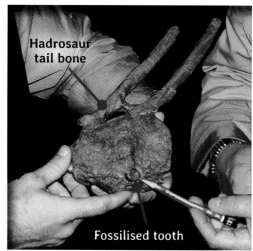

Hadrosaur tail bone

Fossilised tooth

Making a Fossil

At the end of its life, a *T. rex* lies down and dies by the side of a stream.

Insects gather to lay their eggs on the **carcass**.

Belly becomes bloated by gases.

Once a dinosaur died, its body may have rotted in the sun, been washed away in floods or eaten by scavengers. This is why it's very rare to find a complete fossil dinosaur. There were usually only a few bits left to fossilise.

Days pass and the carcass begins to decay. The flesh dries out and shrivels in the sun.

Scavenging animals, such as crocodiles and pterosaurs, eat the rotting flesh.

Big meat-eaters, including other *T. rex*, eat and carry off whole bones and large parts of the carcass.

The rainy season comes and the remains of the *T. rex* are covered by flood water.

Continued

Bones are washed here and there. Some are washed away completely.
The skeleton becomes less and less complete. . . .

The Bones Are Buried

The *Tyrannosaurus rex's* bones are covered by a layer of mud and sand deposited by the floodwaters.

The bones that remain move no further. Above the skeleton, the floodwaters become a stream.

65 Million Years Ago

The stream becomes a river that deposits sand and mud on top of the skeleton. Over tens of thousands of years, more and more layers of sediment build up on top of the bones.

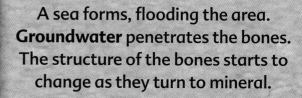

A sea forms, flooding the area. **Groundwater** penetrates the bones. The structure of the bones starts to change as they turn to mineral.

Over millions of years, the layers of sediment are crushed and cemented together, forming limestone rock.

30 Million Years Ago

More and more layers of rock form. Movements in the Earth's crust push the rock upward. High above the skeleton, mountains form. The rocks are twisted and torn by the movements.

The skeleton has become a fossil inside the rock. It is broken and twisted as the rock moves.

2 Million Years Ago

The mountains stop moving and growing.

Wind, rain and snow begin to wear them down.

As thousands of years pass by, the T. rex skeleton moves closer and closer to the surface.

Today

As the rocks around it are worn away, the fossilised skeleton begins to appear.

One day, the tip of a bone is found by accident.

Antarctic Fossils

Fossils of animals and plants can show us how parts of our planet have changed over time.

Today, the rocky land in Antarctica is covered by a sheet of ice that's 1.6 kilometres deep. It is colder than inside a freezer and there are hardly any animals or plants.

But 190 million years ago, Antarctica was very different. The land was covered with forests and meadows. We know this because palaeontologists have found fossilised trees and other plants. They found the fossils on mountainsides where there is less ice. Antarctica was even home to dinosaurs!

Fossilised fern from Antarctica

In 1986, palaeontologists in Antarctica discovered fossils of a herbivorous (plant-eating) dinosaur that they named *Antarctopelta*.

In 1991, scientists found fossils of a 6-metre-long carnivorous (meat-eating) dinosaur, which has been named *Cryolophosaurus*. It had a bony crest on its head and its name means "frozen crest lizard".

During the time of the dinosaurs, Antarctica looked very different.

Let's Experiment

Make Your Own Fossils

It's possible to make your own rocky fossils. It won't take millions of years for these fossils to form, however, just about 30 minutes!

Equipment:
- Leaves, seashells or any object that you want to fossilise
- Plasticine
- Cooking oil
- A strip of cardboard about 2.5 cm wide
- A paper clip
- Plaster of Paris
- A bowl
- Water
- A spoon for mixing

Method:

1 Using your hands, roll out a lump of plasticine so it is flat and smooth.

2 Press a seashell or leaf into the plasticine and then remove it.

3 Rub a little cooking oil into the shape in the plasticine with your fingers.

4 Using the cardboard strip and paper clip, make a little collar, or wall, around the shape.

5 Put some plaster of Paris into the bowl, add some water and start stirring. The mixture should be the thickness of pancake batter with no lumps. Keep adding plaster or water until the mix is right.

6 Spoon or pour the mix into the shape in the plasticine and then fill the cardboard collar with more of the mix.

7 The plaster should set hard in about 30 minutes. Gently touch the plaster to find out if it is dry and hard. If it still feels soft, leave it for another 10 minutes and then try again.

8 When the plaster is hard and dry, gently remove the plasticine from around the model. You will have a fossil-like version of the object you pressed into the plasticine.

Mary Anning:
The Fossil Finder

Mary Anning was a young woman with a passion for fossils who would become a trailblazer for female scientists.

Mary was born in 1799 into a poor family in the seaside town of Lyme Regis, in Dorset. Her parents had 10 children, but only Mary and her brother Joseph survived past their early years.

Mary Anning's father taught her how to carefully chip away at rocks to expose the fossils inside.

Rock hammer

Tray the dog

Mary Anning's fossil shop in Lyme Regis

FOSSIL DEPOT

Mary's father made a humble living from carpentry. To supplement the family's income, he sold objects known as "curiosities" to tourists. The curiosities were actually fossils that he found in rocks that fell from the cliffs. Young Mary helped her father search for fossils, such as ammonites.

When Mary was only 12, her father died. Finding and selling fossils gave Mary a way to help support her family.

In 1811, Mary's brother Joseph found the fossilised skull of a mysterious new creature. Mary then searched for and carefully **excavated** its 5.2-metre-long body. Many local people believed she had discovered a monster! But in fact she had dug up the first-ever *Ichthyosaurus* to be found.

Fossils of ammonites (**extinct** ocean animals)

Mary's Monster

The name *Ichthyosaurus* means fish lizard. Today we know that this animal was a marine reptile – not a fish or a lizard. It lived about 200 million years ago.

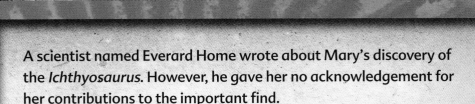

An *Ichthyosaurus* fossil

A scientist named Everard Home wrote about Mary's discovery of the *Ichthyosaurus*. However, he gave her no acknowledgement for her contributions to the important find.

Mary went on to discover many more fossils. She continued to pass on her finds and her clever **theories** about fossils to male scientists in London. But being a woman (at this time in history), she was not allowed to join any scientific societies or have her theories published in scientific books or papers.

Mary's detailed drawing of her *Plesiosaurus* skeleton

Legacy

In the 1800s, Scientists were starting to challenge old views that the world was just thousands of years old (rather than billions of years old as we know today). They also began to realise that there was a time when animals that are now extinct walked and swam on Earth. Mary's work and her fossils influenced this thinking and helped the new science of palaeontology develop.

Today, people all over the world recognise Mary Anning as a **pioneer** for female scientists. She is also a role model for people who feel they are limited by their gender.

Although Mary did not receive full credit for her work when she was alive, we now understand how much of an impact she made with her fascinating fossils.

During her fossil-hunting career, Mary discovered the skeleton of a *Plesiosaurus* and the fossilised bones of a pterosaur (flying reptile) called *Dimorphodon*.

What Is Soil Made Of?

In most places, Earth's rocky land is covered with a layer of soil. But what is soil made of?

Rocks

The main ingredient in soil is sediment, or tiny grains of rock. When wind, rain or melted snow weathers (or wears away) large rocks, tiny bits of rock crumble off and become part of the soil.

A handful of soil may contain bits of rock in many sizes. Some are pebbles the size of grapes. Others are the size of a grain of sugar. And some grains of rock are so small they can only be seen with a microscope.

Grains of rock

Organic Material

Soil is also made of leaves, flowers and other parts of dead plants. An ingredient in soil that was once alive is called **organic matter**. This material **decomposes**, or rots away, and becomes part of the soil. Organic material adds **nutrients** to soil that plants need to grow and be healthy. Plants take in nutrients with their roots.

Water and Air

Soil also contains water and air. In the soil there are many tiny spaces. These tiny tunnels and gaps are often made by worms as they wriggle around underground. Rain and melted snow trickle down into these spaces. Air gets into the soil and collects there, too. Plants take in the water with their roots and underground animals breathe the air.

Dead Bodies and Poo

The dead bodies of insects, birds and other animals are also organic matter. It may take weeks, months or years, but bones, fur, feathers and bits of flesh decompose and become part of the soil. When animals poo, their waste drops to the ground and becomes part of the soil, too.

Microbes on a dead leaf seen under a microscope

Masses of Microbes

There's another ingredient in soil that we cannot see without a powerful microscope – tiny living things called microbes. Microbes help to decompose (break down) organic matter and make it part of the soil. In one handful of garden soil there can be more microbes than there are humans on Earth!

Worm castings

Let's Talk!

What is the sand on a beach made of?
(The answer is on page 32.)

Worm Poo

Worms eat dead plants and soil. When a worm poos, a muddy mixture, called castings, comes out of its tail end. The castings become part of the soil.

Rocks in Our World

There's more rock on our planet than just the many kilometres of it deep below our feet. Rock is also all around us and we use this natural material in many different ways.

These houses have been built with bricks made of limestone.

Slate is used to make tiles for roofs.

Buildings, roads, pavements and skateparks are all built using concrete, which is a mixture of crushed rock, water and cement.

Granite gravel

Rock is crushed to make gravel for paths and gardens.

All the minerals shown here are found in rocks. They are often made into beads for jewellery-making.

Bornite

Red crazy lace agate

Opal

Labradorite

Amethyst

Rose quartz

Carnelian

Let's Talk!

This old, granite gravestone once showed the name and other details of the person who died. What has happened to the words?

Gemstones from Rocks

Some minerals form in crystals that are so colourful, beautiful or rare they are used to make jewellery. Crystals are removed from rocks, cut into shapes and polished. Then they are known as gemstones. Diamonds and rubies are both gemstones.

A diamond in rock

Diamond and ruby earrings

A ruby in rock

Let's Talk!

What kind of mineral do you think is in this rock?

(The answer is on page 32.)

Glossary

canyon
A deep, rocky valley that often has a river running through it.

carcass
A dead body.

classify
To sort into groups that have the same properties or features.

core
The centre of the Earth that is made of solid metal surrounded by an outer core of molten metal.

crust
(of the Earth) The outer layer of the planet that is made of rock.

crystal
A mineral that has formed in a shape that has straight edges and smooth sides, or faces.

decompose
To break down, or rot away, leaving nothing behind but water, gases and minerals.

erosion
The movement, or carrying away, of weathered sediment, usually by waves, the wind, flowing rainwater, melted snow, a stream or a river.

excavate
To dig into the ground, or into rock, to uncover something, such as a fossil.

extinct
No longer in existence; gone forever.

fossil
The hard remains of a living thing that are preserved in rock.

geologist
A scientist who studies rocks.

geology
The study of Earth's structure, rocks and how rocks form.

grain
A tiny piece of something solid, such as rock. For example, sand is made up of tiny grains of rock.

groundwater
Water that has soaked into the ground and collected in the soil or between rocks.

igneous rock
Rock formed from lava (on Earth's surface) and from magma (underground).

lava
Molten magma from inside Earth that has reached the surface, usually during a volcanic eruption.

magma
Rock that has been melted and turned into a thick, super-hot liquid by extreme heat inside Earth.

mantle
The layer inside Earth between the core and the crust.

metamorphic rock
Rock that has changed from one type to another because of extreme heat or pressure.

mineral
A solid substance found in nature that makes up rocks. Quartz, feldspar and metals, such as iron, are all types of minerals.

molten
Turned to liquid by heat.

nutrients
Substances needed by a plant or animal to help it live and grow. For example, the mineral nitrogen is a nutrient that helps plants grow leaves.

ore
A type of rock from which metal can be removed, or extracted.

organic matter
Natural material that was once living or comes from something living — for example, dead leaves and animal poo.

palaeontologist
A scientist who studies animals and plants from the past.

pioneer
The first person (or one of the first) to do something new.

property
A quality that helps to describe what an object or substance is like — for example, shiny or dull, rough or smooth.

scavenge
To feed on dead plants or on dead bodies.

sediment
Tiny pieces of rock that have broken away from a larger rock. Pebbles and grains of sand are both types of sediment.

sedimentary rock
Rock made from many layers of sediment that have been pressed together under extreme pressure so they join and become rock.

soil
A layer of (usually) black or brown material that forms the upper layer of Earth where plants grow. Soil is mostly made from tiny particles of rock and rotted organic matter.

tectonic plates
Giant, jigsaw-like pieces of Earth's crust.

theory
An idea or belief that is based on limited information. A theory can be proved with evidence.

volcano
An opening in Earth's crust that allows magma onto the surface. Over time, as rock forms from the magma (lava), it creates a mountain.

weathering
The breaking off and wearing away of sediment from rock, usually by the wind, rain, snow or waves.

Index

Answers

Page 27:
Sand is made of sediment (tiny bits of rock). When waves crash against rocky cliffs, sediment breaks off and falls into the water. Sediment also gets carried by rivers out to sea or blown there by the wind. This sediment gets washed up on land and forms beaches. Sand also contains tiny pieces of shell and skeleton from dead ocean animals such as crabs, mussels, corals and sea urchins.

Page 29:
The mineral is gold. Gold is also a metal. It is sometimes found in rocks. About 90 tonnes of the rock (or enough to fill five large dump trucks) would produce one teaspoon of gold.